# The Black Ensemble Theater

## by Penelope Reese

Scott Foresman
is an imprint of

PEARSON

Glenview, Illinois • Boston, Massachusetts • Mesa, Arizona
Shoreview, Minnesota • Upper Saddle River, New Jersey

**Photographs**
Every effort has been made to secure permission and provide appropriate credit for photographic material. The publisher deeply regrets any omission and pledges to correct errors called to its attention in subsequent editions.

Unless otherwise acknowledged, all photographs are the property of Pearson Education, Inc.

Photo locators denoted as follows: Top (T), Center (C), Bottom (B), Left (L), Right (R), Background (Bkgd)

**CVR** © Black Ensemble Theater; **1** © Black Ensemble Theater; **3** Erin Donnelley Photography; **4** © Black Ensemble Theater; **6** (L) © John Springer Collection/Corbis, (R) © Bettmann/Corbis, (C) © Bettmann/Corbis; **7** © Black Ensemble Theater; **8** © SuperStock, Inc./SuperStock; **9** (T) © Bettmann/Corbis, (B) © Marc Brasz/Corbis; **10** © Dennis Galante/Corbis; **11** © Black Ensemble Theater; **12** (L) © Black Ensemble Theater, (R) © Black Ensemble Theater; **13** © Black Ensemble Theater; **14** © Black Ensemble Theater; **15** © Ken Simmons/Black Ensemble Theater; **16** Corbis; **19** © Black Ensemble Theater.

ISBN 13: 978-0-328-39481-4
ISBN 10:     0-328-39481-5

4 5 6 7 8 9 10  V0FL  14 13 12 11

Chicago's Black
Ensemble Theater

On a quiet street in Chicago's Uptown neighborhood, there is excitement in the air. Play practice is in session at the city's famous Black Ensemble Theater. The troupe, or group of actors, is rehearsing a show called *Sounds So Good...Makes You Wanna Holler*. It's just one show in a long line of musicals this company has put on over the years. The theater has existed since 1976.

3

*Sounds So Good… Makes You Wanna Holler* at the Black Ensemble Theater

   *Sounds So Good…Makes You Wanna Holler* is about a clash between a father and son. The son dreams of making it big in the music business. His father doesn't think it's a good idea, though. He wants his son to go into business—any business but music. So the son must decide what to do.

Like the other shows put on at the Black Ensemble Theater, this show centers around music. Shows at this theater highlight the work of some of America's greatest black musicians. But *Sounds So Good...Makes You Wanna Holler* has a new twist.

Sammy Davis, Jr.

Aretha Franklin

Billie Holiday

Earlier shows at the Black Ensemble Theater usually included music by African American artists from the past. The theater showcased the music of Billie Holiday, Sammy Davis, Jr., and countless other singers from previous decades. Several shows have told the life stories of famous black music-makers of the past.

Productions at the Black Ensemble Theatre feature music from the past, such as this production of *Don't Make Me Over*.

The Motown record label was especially popular in the 1960s. Motown churned out one hit record after another. Motown's list of artists included many great soul singers. This type of soul music became widely known as the "Motown sound." The label got its name because the company was located in Detroit, Michigan. Detroit was the center of the car-making industry, and it was often called "Motor City," or "Motown."

*Sounds So Good…Makes You Wanna Holler* features music by artists from the past, such as The Temptations and Aretha Franklin. But the show also features newer music. The show includes musical **arrangements** of hit songs from popular artists such as John Legend.

John Legend

*Sounds So Good…Makes You Wanna Holler* blends sounds from yesterday and today.

Sounds So Good…Makes You Wanna Holler lets the audience play a part in the show too. During the show, the singers perform the old and new music. Then the audience gets to decide on their favorite!

9

# Behind the Scenes

How does the Black Ensemble Theater keep churning out one hit show after another? It takes a lot of time and effort.

First, there is the playwright who writes the **script** for the show. Then, a director is hired to make sure the playwright's vision comes across onstage. Next, actors are chosen to play each part in the show. Finally, rehearsals begin!

Many things happen backstage before the show can begin.

There are many people who work backstage too. There are costume designers, set designers, and makeup artists. A show also needs people to handle the lighting and sound. Other workers keep track of the many costumes and props being used onstage.

With so many people working together, things can get complicated. Personalities may clash and **arguments** may break out. The show might hit a **snag** that slows everything down. These types of problems sometimes keep a play from ever having its opening night.

Black Ensemble Theater founder Jackie Taylor

An ensemble theater has an advantage when problems arise. The members of an ensemble theater often work together on different shows over many years. So they get to know each other well, and they learn how to work together. More importantly, the members of an ensemble theater usually share a common vision, or goal. Having a common vision is important when working as a team.

The goal of the Black Ensemble Theater is to produce shows that lift people's spirits. Its founder, Jackie Taylor, started the theater because she wanted to show African Americans in positive roles.

Jackie Taylor in a Chicago production of *Death and the King's Horsemen* in 1979.

Ms. Taylor is a playwright, director, and actor. While she was working in Hollywood, she found that some movies showed African Americans in negative roles. Black characters were often shown as **dishonest** or worse. So she returned to her hometown of Chicago and opened her own theater.

Jackie Taylor has won many awards for her work as playwright, director, and actor. Here she receives the 2006-2007 Black Theater Alliance Award. She won the trophy for Best Direction of a Musical for *Memphis Soul: The Story of Stax Records*. Ms. Taylor has written and directed many of the shows at the Black Ensemble Theater.

Ms. Taylor started the Black Ensemble Theater with a loan of just $1,200. She didn't have a lot of money, but she was determined to make it a success. Her idea was to create plays that would bring people together. She wanted every show to celebrate the human spirit and bring joy to everyone in the audience. And of course she wanted music— lots of it!

In *The House that Rocked* (2004), actors portrayed recording artists Little Richard, Fats Domino, and Chuck Berry.

Her vision helped set the tone of every musical produced by the Black Ensemble Theater. And her idea drew in others who wanted to achieve the same goals. People got behind Ms. Taylor in many ways. They gave her **advice**, funds, and offered their time and talents.

Today, Ms. Taylor's vision still guides every stage production. And people are flocking to see her shows. The theater is now a million-dollar company. Ms. Taylor and her theater also have earned many awards over the years.

# Reaching Out

People from all across Chicago come to the Black Ensemble Theater. Sold-out shows draw men, women, and young people of every race and profession.

The theater has earned its place in the community, and its goals have expanded. Much of the music in these shows has its roots in the music of enslaved workers during the 1800s. Some **descendants** of those workers are onstage and backstage today. The theater group is sharing this music—and the stories of African American life—with everyone. But the members of the theater group are also reaching out in other important ways.

In the 1800s, enslaved field workers in the American South created "call and response" or "holler back" songs as they worked.

A big part of the Black Ensemble Theater is giving back to the community. The theater offers many programs to children and adults. Two of these are designed especially for elementary school students, their parents, and their teachers. These are "Plays With a Purpose" and "Strengthening the School with Theater Arts."

# Black Ensemble Theater Outreach Programs

| Program Name | Program's Aim |
| --- | --- |
| Strengthening the School Through Theater Arts | To teach theater arts to elementary school students |
| Arts for Parents in School Communities | To help parents get involved in their children's schools |
| New Directions | To help teens build self-esteem through theater arts |
| Community Access Program | To provide free and discounted theater tickets |
| Theater for Special Men and Women | To teach theater arts to developmentally challenged and disabled adults |
| Plays with a Purpose | To teach children through fun, interactive plays |
| Summer Training in the Technical Arts | To teach technical skills to teens |
| Black Playwrights Initiative | To help young African American playwrights develop their scripts |

The cast from *The Other Cinderella*.

Many people may have thought that Ms. Taylor's theater was too small to make a big difference. But that didn't stop her from following her dream. She was able to find a group of people who wanted to help her. Each night, the group entertains the audience with uplifting stories and lively music. But that's not all. They continue to keep spirits up even after the show is over.

# Glossary

advice *n.* an opinion about what should be done

argument *n.* discussion by persons who disagree

arrangements *n.* plans; preparations

descendants *n.* offspring; children

dishonest *adj.* showing lack of honesty or fairplay

script *n.* manuscript of a play, movie, or radio or TV show

snag *n.* a hidden or unexpected obstacle